Through My Eyes from The Sky

Joel Harris

Revised cover edition 2020

For any use of content
Contact for information:
Email: joelawharris@gmail.com
Facebook : king atterberry7
Instagram: king_atterberry

Isbn: 978-1-7352952-8-2
Library of Congress
Copyrighted ©2017

Table of Contents

MIND

through my eyes from the sky!!

Matter fact lets spit I'm equiped making moves.
This brother does what he does I'm just in tune with live grooves.
Adapt to different work I put it in the carry-on.
Just shoot me a verse I'm not trying to hear a song.
Dance around life whatever way mainly I two-step.
Hit me with some logic, and I'll stamp it with some concepts.
This man gets his weight up and flexes many skills.
When its time to reveal I keep it real when I reveal.
Been locked in housebound until I found the underground.
I'm from the city relocated to the shore inside a small town.
Aint nothing to a traveler I get in where I fit in.
Regained righteousness from my days living in sin.
Got the focus of a young guard, looking up to real god.
Hands together head held high I set a new mark.
My road is complex the way I walk on many paths.
Cant track what I do unless you use a holy compass.
Step into the eye of a storm even if I'm warned.
Embrace my calm I got hands that show cosmic palms.
Lifeline irregular this fellow love the cold weather.
Body temperature handled I rep the 7th letter.
True and living giving even getting never switching.
I'm a hundred never fronting that's why all still sitting.

enter the moment

All praises to the most high, lift me up till I'm sky high.
Rest in peace to the old guy, nowadays meet the new guy.
Location of me at the shore in cape may; I reside on the north side.
They pass me by, the god in my eyes I levitate before my demise.
Grinding hard from a cloth I was cut, can't dupe that old fabric.
Challenging dolphins and rabbits feed them bait and raw cabbage.
Speak to the source keep steady on course; gods plan is a big one.
Gave life to the stars the moon and the sun, my physical self is at one.
Some of the people that lost in this world can't connect on my level.
Dancing around with ill devils and rebels, I refuse just to settle.
Prayers on deck spiritual circle embody the earth and its issues.
Don't let these problems get to you; faith is the only thing to fix you.
Walking and talking speak in a language meditate on the fly.
Shine bright with my light when I'm ready take flight way up on the high.
I'm way up on the high, looking below at these zeros.
Ride clouds on earth soft as pillows praising god for his heroes.
Praising God for his heroes, I'm blessed in ways unnatural.
Do things that I want don't really have only to advance to catch you.
Nights be so dark on evenings I work they planning my exit quick.
Whoever they mix along with the tricks go and prepare my crucifix.
Treat me like Jesus with Romans in tow my eyes close to the known.
When I go back home, I return to your zone refreshed I'm fully atoned.
Sinfull of all that disgrace the heart of godchild in the flesh.
Sorry you tried your best cause you're
stressed on life and can't accept.

It's guud

Mind-body and soul absent thoughts from the flesh.
The will of God at its best nothing more nothing less.
Allow everything natural to exist day to day.
Battle all challenges with the way we kneel and pray.
A lot of thoughts we hold on to so hard to let things go.
In order for us to grow to raise up from below.
Even a dead man can sing a song not heard by everyone.
Reach out and touch the heart of someone and have a little fun.
Smile a little hug a little kiss and say hello.
Leave the past in a glass bottle enjoy a new tomorrow.
The present now shows your presence when its due.
Focus on the original and know precisely what to do.
Stay balanced on the wave remain grounded when you flow.
Knock loud on the world door and let people know.
I'm here to take a position when I stand to check me out.
It's not about word of mouth when you have specific clout.

Another way

Checking the hands on my timepiece verbal war end with peace.
Made a call to my niece, she caught her boyfriend hiding cheese.
Chick that she saw in the hallway of her front door.
Rolling up that peter raw wicked in it's on paw.
Indonesia woman speaking to me what's going on.
Built strong go the distance standing on the right from wrongs.
Motivated by the books I read one day train my seed.
Digest the knowledge if he learned find himself under siege.
Drowning in a bad sea, life shit happening.
Daddy got an idea resurrect that real action.
Blasting off technology everybody hooked on it.
Write some crazy lyrics to a beat no hook on it.
Melody and rhythm that's the tune that I move to.
Dancing to an old school two-step my father's groove.
Got mommy in my system hoping to see my lane change.
What I love about myself is that I never feel ashamed.
Gods comfort placing holy hands on my spirit guide.
The soul takes a cosmic ride heaven side you and I.
Past life Jesus Christ thinking with his consciousness.
Best for me my homegirl chilled me from some nonsense.
Lift the dark keep the light use sight day or night.
Walking with that pure bright apparel dressed in all white.
Place me in that circle of feel-good affection.
Spiritual connection real blessing scripture lesson.
Hold to heart here my dear baby I'm in good space.
Protect my place walk with righteousness in or out of state.
See the man adult riser planetary watch exist.
Earth shift of its axis know the world switch.

FOLLOW THE PATH

They said my manners be to fly the way my interactions be.
I'm brolic well-polished everything solid notices me.
Nickname cosmic exist within time and space.
My energy radiates from the universe state to state.
Hands help the people never one to hurt the righteous.
The word for a word which is a tyrant lets flow who got the tightest.
Even with arthritis run circles on track fielders.
My aura is the healer keep it buck fifty more real.
Then a hundred im feeling strange feelings in my stomach.
Intuition is going crazy I'm learning joining the east summit.
Mix with the beautiful, outgoing spirits.
The way that I feel it, I can no longer conceal it.
Ways of the world changing god asking for payments.
Sacrifices in life you name it, and he may ordain it.
Awakened in the mind of the people on a journey.
Holla if you heard all of my words nodd if you hear me.
Handshake the brother hug and kiss the sisters.
Communicate with listeners ignore all the whispers.

KING ATTERBERRY

Put them on blast let them feel the wrath I'm dropping an avalanche.
If all really want to take a chance dance and ride an ambulance.
Aint nothing sweet on this street my heat carries sun rays.
Call it summertime fire blaze let me stay where they body lay.
Hands make the day seem longer than it is already.
the mp3 player is rocking reggae rock your life away.
A different side of me is not spiritual check the residue.
Attitude igloo whether it kick you or it hit you.
Lessons on the fly respect OGs from the seventies.
My thoughts become deadly playing a gangster style medley.
I let it rain heavy and steady when taking pot shots.
Hot hands Harris keep the pot in a specific slot.
The discipline of the old easterners is how I live.
So excuse my negative that was my old mentality shit.
Now I spill a convoy to the conscious mind of any dude.
Nickname Joe cool one of many that I style and groom.
Next time I give a piece of mind contemplating my thought.
Forget whatever you think or thought my emotions are raw.

get em joe2

When they come for my neck, I turtle myself into a shell hardback.
Coast clear I throw shots back big difference is facts.
Fabrication is what they breed god's love is what I breathe.
On my left arm is a cross that bears Jesus blood so all eyes can see.
Fear no one, state I'm from anything get done to give the drummer some.
Lessons I learned in sessions receive the blessings hail the sun.
No sky is falling why they are creeping crawling like a roach.
Shine that light on they approach death to all now your eggs poached.
What you say and think is Gemini who you are fooling on the do side.
All these crabs die it a far cry when your levels dry.
Buck fifty on the matters that you speak shut down your streak.
Excuse me as I pass gas free handed as I take a leak.
Pardon me if I don't talk especially acting ill to me.
What comes around goes back around boomerang no frisbees.
Lyrically I'm a fool with it talented gifted and fresh to be wit.
Hold my peoples down connect with sets king Atteberry did it.

get bizzy

On em ayo, the flow doesn't stop the wave just started.
Push the whip to any damn block double park it.
Exit out be on the corner chopping it up.
Ears still are on the street I play the cut.
Sidebar falls back when were you relevant.
Challenge anybody my bars keep you hella bent.
Notation to the world fuck is you talking about.
I only deal real ground facts instead of word of mouth.
Break down barriers locate the carriers.
Haters work miraculous ain't nobody passing us.
Fuckery and mockery delivered in the same boat.
Crying motherfuckers, they duck us wishing they had hope.
Playing cloak and daggers, I wonder what really matters.
Wave runners are standing well balanced against disasters.
Only time will tell if the people can hold a note.
Drop in a box in the ocean and make a toast.

I DONT KNOW

Does she ever still remember me with mental telepathy.
There's a change in society my thoughts again bother me.
Am I chasing waterfalls or searching for lost calls?
Believing in the cause or going through withdraw.
Maybe something I saw or missed when I was chilling.
Knocked from my position while handling my children.
The man that I am only real women can see.
Perhaps she isn't for me yet still a possibility.
Giving it all I got as I turn it up a notch.
Managing my timeslots, throughout my eye shots.
My thoughts reach the source from the moment I shut down.
Wake up to binary sounds and still feel earthbound.
Signals to out of space I already sealed my fate.
Waiting on a date resemble case inside my state.
The mind is designed many different frames working.
I'm steady working for sure and one day close a curtain.

LIES VERSUS THE TRUTH

Some of the stories don't add up suspect in its own right.
There's a difference in the daytime than exposure in the night
life.
Don't you know the streets talk where the peeps walk now?
There's no circus in our town yet still I see a bunch of clowns.
Frowns upside down excuse me what you mad about.
What happened to your clout, it's funny how you run your
mouth.
Thought you were getting dough serving John McEnroe.
Penny pinching on the low creeping sneaking on your toes.
We bifocal your steez please we see the real you.
Old Magoo ties your shoe witness how we break the news.
Teleport facts off the track we in the field daily.
Aint a word connected keep it stepping god won't ever fail me.
Whatever that your selling telling you don't even have got.
A pot to piss in the window to throw it out mark your spot.
For all the ear droppers tear dropper's drama rockers.
Nosey eye clockers we got some real kept in our lockers.

ocean and the bay

I used to go with the flow but now I'm under time management.
Move so fast through the week can't tell where the time went.
When I chill, I'm in the white whip headed here and there.
Destination I don't know I just drive feeling the air.
Find a place to park in the light never in the dark.
Re-Introduce me to the streets holding off on the bark.
True indeed a king in his own right commission his duty.
Wonder who is he, son of a universe truly.
Man of god going hard no squad crew or team.
Solo activist extreme measures poetry feigns.
Carry light through visions of thoughts seeing a caper.
Working my jobs as if I'm limited to extra paper.
Givers and takers don't the test the hands and legs of me.
My legacy can be biographic in New York city.
In cape may I break the barriers on jobs with work ethics.
Bullshit I just forget it and let my lord get it.

out there with no fear

Bring me back to the days mentally when my pops died.
Same time my mom's lied I still cried and got high.
Rolled up and twisted all the weed I got my hands on.
Tall cans of O.E guzzling got it on the arm.
Young dude going through it hard I'm like fuck that.
Verbal war with mom duke grams said fall back.
I chilled resurrect my father spirit deal with her.
Respect the womb I came from treating her like no monster.
Accepted who she was, allow her to fix herself.
Blame nobody else so now I ride waves with no belt.
Speak with specific tone still respectful but observant.
Cant treat me like a servant ma dukes I don't deserve it.
All she ever did was speak about things she is going to does.
Didn't hold on to it, so I said ok bye nu nu.
The mentality was seven different ways I dealt with her.
When she needed me, I was there because she was my
mother.

see

Thinking back to my days by the Hudson riverside drive.
My spirit was alive when it survived how did life die.
Expecting not see what all the time was there.
Almost lost my mind but came back to re-align.
The pressure just alone had the heart pumping fast.
Took a glance at opportunity went home and laughed.
Next day apply courage and strength to the wave.
Sent a present to the cause as I stood tall and brave.
Cash limited, but the effects were very huge.
Allied we all cool after hour brews.
Pictures painted verbally and physically no canvas.
Weather is looking bad all these trees losing branches.
Unite as a team, a set full of go-getters.
Making life better creator keeping us together.
Active in practice choose a skillset out the archive.
Catalog serious no wonder I walk on by.

BODY

a cosmic thing

Ride that wave baby it feels good to see your style.
The way your eyes look inside of mine I'm enjoying your smile.
Talk to me baby where my heart uses to love.
Allow me to touch your soul and hug your spirit.
Place my hands on yours is this verbal intercourse.
Let my mental touch yours and you touch mine breaking the law.
Lighting so dim you let me in to check the fuse.
Without anything to lose can I exploit the use of my tools.
I'm handy to assist as long you don't resist.
If it's your wish, I don't persist its ok, but I can sniff.
The smell of your aura got me drowning in your water.
From the first time, I felt your magnetism I adored ya.
Sweet air I breathe off the surface of your plane.
Things never were the same as I changed astral lane.
What I think and you think the divine match our space.
Whatever the case lets speak or just trace.
Steps to move each other to that moment co-exist.
Trust our energy and presence as I memorize your lips.
Cover me with your radiance engulf me with yourself.
Align your essence with my presence trap ourselves in one belt.

fresh

Out of nowhere, she appeared in the form of a goddess.
She held out her hand and told me please don't be modest.
Explaining my humble manner so that she will know.
Blinded by her glow, she picks me up when I am low.
Kissed me on the cheek and saw a mirrored reflection.
Took deep breath as I asked for a lesson.
So kind of her to show me many different ways.
The concepts of loyalty and honesty I ate.
Such feelings so deep that makes you always think of her.
Anything outside of love to me is just a blur.
Although inanimate still compassionate and cool.
I get the greatest sensation when I always think of you.
Mrs.TLC is very beautiful to me.
always in my heart where my eyes can't see

Hello

As I walk this world in the distance, hold my thoughts upon an angel.
Same feelings that I have when I see a beautiful flower.
Guard her field of health with strong prayers to god.
Holding my hands together under sunlight to get charged.
The energy that I feel from emotions concealed.
When the time is ready, everything will be revealed.
The smile of the most exotic picture holding grace.
Examining her presence visions of roses in a vase.
Whether verbal or just a certain look that tells a story.
If I asked her to take my heart, I know she holds it for me.
Secure its location where it won't be easy to find.
You can dig the deepest hole or find mountains to climb.
But search for a clue around horizons everywhere.
The glow that she wears will have my heart reappear.
Hello

Next Time Around

Allow yourself to be pampered by the words that I say.
Take a walk and hold my hands its date night at the bay.
Be at ease and feel the breeze as the waves hit the shore.
Open the door to natures law is a mi Amor.
When the last time you felt so good without touching.
The ancient way of hugging and loving displaying something.
Gently kiss your wrist and lips with no intent.
Absorbing your lovely scent caress your face astonishing.
Let's catch the fever bash in some flavor of each other.
Be that special kind of friend who can melt you like butter.
Freshen up your emotions and take your heart.
Rekindle the spark brighten your light if dim or dark.
Your chico my Chica when I don't see you, I miss you.
Pretending around people that we cordial and civil.
The woman that you are very appealing to me.
Ever a possibility you bring the man out to be.
Touching your fingertips showing what you can get.
Getting caught in each other's mix till we both lovesick.
Curing each other lonely days can be great.
Enticing each other wave placing ourselves in gods rays.
Sunshine piece of mind stays in line until its time.
You tell me that you want to be more than would fine.
enjoy your read

where we at

Let me hold you in my arms so I can read your feelings.
Bring your conscious to a point where my heart is revealing.
There's something inside of me that comes out when you are around.
I'm enjoying your tone of voice due to beautiful sounds.
The way that you express yourself is loud and very clear.
Even when I see your picture closeness is in the air.
Breathe life into moments allow nature to take its course.
Take my time and let the source bring out a greater force.
Love on you with no hands becoming a better friend.
Dedication inside like your man or husband.
Send you words like gifts on Christmas open it up.
Tender Roni buttercup you know was sup when I am up.
Trust what I touch with no luck I'm in your view.
As long as we stay in tune, we keep the old with the new.

here we go

Ayo, she tastes like candy, my nickname cameo.
Make a guest appearance in her life my story untold.
Walk a path real bright, but she loves when I'm in flight.
I can travel destinations just meet me off the pike.
Hands touch her body strong and soft no doubt.
Fingers rub her lips because she knows what I'm about.
Kiss the clouds for heaven's sake asking god to hold me down.
I'm the new dude in town besides I jus hit the ground.
She is showing me around introducing me as L.
We are hanging out talking and laughing stories to tell.
I'm fascinated by the area multi-environment.
It's getting late im is wondering where the hell the time went.
But I got other plans to take photos out at night.
Caress the moon with my eyes oh yeah, I'm feeling right.
Its all about compassion caring and being cool.
Let's see how I can move, and I don't have a point to prove.
Whether Philly, dc, Baltimore or new yiddy.
This is just a poem cause I'm feeling very silly.

It's all good

Met Mary at 5west pub eating alone.
One hour before I left my home and my throne.
Eye contact we shared as I came through the door.
Was a universal moment, so I had to explore.
Sat across from her table enjoying appetizers.
Shot a smile to her smirk trying to start a fire.
Gave her a wink just to see what she think.
Asked her if we could link and share a nice drink.
Invitation taken ordered two island teas.
We both felt at ease speaking the language of the east.
Asked about my pendants and stones around my neck.
I said woman I'm a king something you can expect.
She said really I said baby I'm from New York.
With that old school talk and an eighty-one walk.
Laughter in the air another waiter appeared.
her hand I grabbed paid the tab because we both love the air

next time around

Expression of her heart what she desires but hasn't found.
The beauty of the sound inside her voice keeps me crowned.
King of her deepest emotions soulfully we are one.
My goddess in the light shines upon me like the sun.
Caress her brown skin lightly touch her lips.
Arms around her waist as my palms rest on her hips.
Look into her eyes form a smile without a word.
The reflection of affection is a milestone she deserves.
Kiss her earlobe whisper words inside her ear.
Her reaction brings a tear to my eyes but disappear.
Examine each other passion cautiously pursuing.
All the things we do we in tune while we are grooving.
Massage her tired feet till she slowly closes her eyes.
She is not even my lady and I'm, not even her guy.
Respect each other's ways as we lay in harmony.
What is supposed to be is naturally her and me.
No ties but we enjoy connected feelings like the source.
Signals never crossed so nobody takes a loss.
It's all right where we stand bondwoman and man.

WHAT'S NEXT

As the evening time emerge as the sun goes away.
The moon comes out to play with its beauty on display.
Whichever way she models her structure we still love her.
Showing her beautiful self, emotionally some suffer.
Trying to understand how she appears with bright light.
Deep into the night, her aura is so right.
Not a mixed glitch, the energy of her life is so fresh.
Through my eyes from the sky, I feel her presence in my flesh.
Mentally I'm aware of how it affected and infected.
Absorb in any sections of my body it still pressing.
When she leaves im quite sad, upset and not mad.
All the moments that we have seem always to make me brag.
Until we pass each other meet again signs deep within.
We entertain deep space until the galaxy defend.

Yes

Let me look into your eyes and take a mental picture.
Let me feel your heartbeat after the hug I'm a kisser.
Can we speak in the tongue as the French do and see?
How many blasts of energy can bring a shield of harmony?
My grey skies are blue now that I saw and met you.
Can I bless you and touch you make love and not fuck you?
Caress those pretty thighs that got me feeling high.
Take your mind on a trip past the atmosphere and rise.
We both in outer space open case on our pace.
Set up a home base and call it our love place.
Feel around your physical till your spirit speaks to mine.
Allow our soul to intertwine and see our soul start to shine.
The way I kiss your body while you're on me HD.
The possibility becomes a reality for you and me.
Kiss both lips for pleasure enter the world forever.
Hold heat together control the weather and bless you.

Thank You2

When im alone in my room, im having holographic visions.
You are standing in my doorway smiling ready for kissing.
Big hugs you give call it the Saturday special.
God I'm very pleased that you sent Chica to rescue.
A man in need of a very special friend.
Love to love her I can feel the energy that you send.
Absorb what is given so caring and that is deep.
When you text, I hear you speak, your voice a memory to me.
Nothing feels better than knowing what you have.
I can see myself washing your back in a bubble bath.
Afterward a nice massage full body, so you rest.
You deserve the best service from the hands that are blessed.
Place my hands on your back rub you gently till you sleep.
I think about you every day and every night when I'm sleep.

SOUL

send it to god

Now I have to flow without a style on this verse.
Entering a different turf without absorbing the dirt.
The playing field is a high level of the game is unique.
Out your window takes a peak, at this man in the street.
The life I lead enchanted by the past life souls.
Story unfolds or somewhat is told to be cold.
The reality of this I give the scriptures a look.
Searching through some holy books, as I stay getting hooked.
It's about the knowledge, wisdom and pure understanding.
Fly about on different routes where I stop there's a landing.
Salute the brother with the wings of an angel in god sight.
Using the power of great might and keeping my mind right.
All my recollection from souls that were before me.
Gaining gods glory my circle really adore me.
high points of shitting out thoughts that were suggested.
Wasnt the right suggestion, so I learned another lesson.
The bad guy the good guy back to being the why guy.
Aint is giving a try I'm Christ conscious high.
So I re-emerge my thinking distance off assumptions.
Believe me when I'm coming I'm gunning for what ain't trumping.
Salute my allegiance to the team that knows better.
My king dreams of seeing things better will never sever.

two sides to everyone

Turn off the light and see a brother in the dark.
Illuminating with a Christ conscious no heart.
How the hell is he alive, they thought the god really died.
Resurrected off the tears, you didn't see the angel cry.
The pain was in the air the Almighty saw the crime.
My past life was dirty, so they changed me this time.
But karma got a way of swinging back and forth damn.
Too late to be the man that measure sand hears i am.
Searching for that sun-dial dealing wit the power now.
The community of praying people lets all keep our heads
bowed.
I love my people who like the people they my people.
The link to compassion can't be broken or seen through.
We all chant the mantra that displays a certain aura.
Drinking from a cup feel the source inside the water.
Awake from a dream state of deaf dumb and blind.
The lines in my rhymes show a sign from
the divine

Poem of aww

Praise the most high no lie prays until your soul feel.
Words from the ancient seal that keep your whole body still.
Mental mind focused righteous thoughts come across well.
Only time will tell if the lord rings your doorbell.
Open your heart to compassion love and honesty.
Always going forward cant look back at whats suppose to be.
Talk god walk with God also be on your guard.
Devil got plans for you playing in his backyard.
Can't be mad at people allow the lord to handle it.
A hero isn't nothing but a sandwich therefor banishes it.
Stay equip see the light if its dark starts a spark.
Have to live large be in charge when times are hard.
Momma use to say be accountable for things you do.
There's nothing really new when you're feeling down and blue.
Sunny days are coming breaking the grey skies glooming.
Whatever way make your day bright without consuming.
Bad that is looming killing your peaceful aura.
Cleanse your spirit every Sunday wash in holy water.
Powerful as the word is rain on me on me daily.
Thanks to the blood of Christ respect the Virgin Mary.

over here and over there

I see my world as an ocean my brain is the ore.
My head is the canoe, I'm exploring to find a shore.
Only mirage insight into my vision is what I'm seeking.
Sweet voices that keep me dreaming of myself I'm barely speaking.
Surrounded by mass water my destination plagued.
Asking God to save the day or I drown by different waves.
So I pray and set the stage on a high note through meditation.
No revelation just patience archived in situations.
Time is wasted on thoughts my real feelings torn.
All the signs and symbols warn about the calm before the storm.
Mystified by a cry in human form did I die.
Before I rise check my eyes, please don't ask a reason why.
There's a purpose to the next phase of life that I been told.
Kneeling down as my hands fold and architect a show.
My performance in the virtual reality is done.
open the door and be aware of the land from which I come

moving along

Sign of the times is here, feeling the presence that's near.
The only divine I fear keeping my thoughts aware and sincere.
Cant hold a man back that move forward in life as it change.
Left the pain in a holy drain resurrect what is good and so plain.
God knows what my intentions be as I take a stand living free.
Walking down a narrow path singing songs so heavenly.
Full of joy and excitement as i observe scenes so nice.
Doing things that are right within the eyes that see my sight.
Land of the shore forever more has me thinking out the box.
Close to those that love my heart remain solid as a rock.
Rainbow emotions harvest a new way to live.
What I have to give is priceless here my dear a bridge.

Heaven's child

Beautiful flower from a section of my homeland.
True essence of a love child well blossomed for a true man.
Only he that acknowledge the nature of a rose.
Feel the emotion in your heart from you head to your toes.
Handle with care express unconditional affection.
It's a blessing to admire embrace god's unique connection.
Invisible smile long as the Nile check out her style.
Never wild versatile there is no limit on really how.
Search high and low on your mind not hard to find.
One of a kind well aligned open the heart and feel her shine.
The glow incomparable lovable and loyal.
Take care of her soil making sure you up and close to.
From a distance, she consistently presents at any moment.
Whatever you are atoned with better see what she owned with.
Purified goddess heavens daughter is living life.
Whatever wrong feels right just pray for her thru the night.
Hoping her day's wonderful expressions of gratitude.
Give her petals no attitude good talking creates a mood.
"Just for you" By Joel

alright now

Give me strawberry thoughts with blueberry affection.
Point me in the right direction where I can see the love connection.
If a train really exists and a stairwell to heaven.
I will be sitting at the station studying my scripture lessons.
Stepping up always keeping my hand on the railing.
Perhaps rent a yacht, so I can go smooth sailing.
Face the east when I'm talking to god and his angels.
Copped a pair of Buddhist bangles so I can channel every angle.
Die for what I believe so dedicated to breathing.
All I need is the god vision to see indeed.
I heed all that's accepted on blind faith no question.
what I profess I suggest nothing less feel blessings

dream girl

Long day at work but it's cool how she feels me.
I'm aligned with the stars full moons don't scare me.
Helps the communication with the star in my universe.
Striving every year and celebrate on August 1st.
I'm a child of the sun energetic and charismatic.
Got that inner circle power true friends magnetic.
Day of rest I try my best revive my flesh with consciousness.
Mental thoughts I do digest no ugliness inside my chest.
Carry god armor cross on my left as I walk right.
3rd vision sight autopilot when I'm in flight.
Telepathic charm expresses to her on planes astral.
Any way I see her all love for now casual.
Close my eyes visualize a future on a high level.
Massage her spirit when I feel it that if she wants the medal.

matter of fact

Traveling across state line destination unknown.
Trying to find that one home that I saw in a dream zone.
Setting is beautiful trees and flowers are so exotic.
No maps and roads on gps where I stop are where I get started.
Mission after my own that I saw when meditating.
Godsend me the location where you find that woman waiting.
Wearing a skirt and blouse feet footed inside of sandals.
Wondering to myself if this is real life can I handle.
Pause the car at this diner by a lake with pretty scenery.
Thoughts of tea and bagels with cream cheese sound good to me.
Stranger to this town, so my presence brings a stare.
Slacks and button-up shirt Stacy Adams at this time I wear.
But I'm African American is sitting eating amongst these white folks.
I see this hostess very polite to me noticing that I'm, not dead broke.
Out of my wallet, I pass a twenty she changes me back, and I dip.
Walk along the side of the lake view this is perfect.
Sit down on a bench close my eyes to say a prayer.
Sunshine in my eyes I focus on my layers.
There's multitudes of what I view to see where I am going.
Home beneath the trees with a bed of flowers god be showing.

ME AND MY FRIEND

Let me begin by telling a tale of two people.
Opposite attraction of a man and woman equal.
Different in they own right studying course of god.
Living states apart although connecting through the heart.
Her beauty is displayed from a glow an earth angel.
His ancient dialect is projected from stones and angles.
Elevation modified through righteous written text.
The wave they each ride is from the tenements and jects.
Grind and hustle hard making every day a first.
Never seeming last, stay on the path for what it's worth.
Eyes are the window to the soul let it be told.
The image that they hold from the creator is of gold.
Yet we all have flaws with open doors receiving more.
In life, we headed for, what the Lord has in store.
Believing in each other up lighted and enlightened.
Until the day we meet again talking through all-star lighting.
ME AND MY FRIEND

monetary moment

Walk to her house from two blocks I parked.
That spark in my heart got me drifting apart.
Thoughts on a dinner and a flick of tv.
Send my mind in a daze am I going crazy.
Knock on her door bright smile on her face.
The backside of my fingers gives her cheeks a slight trace.
After a long embrace that's exactly what takes place.
From the flights I walked up, I need a slow pace.
It's the lips that I taste open the gate of our care.
Only voices we hear is our tone in the air.
Sit on the couch smelling the food she prepared.
Her apparel is tight I don't mean to stare.
Its nights like this that set the mood really good.
Maturity well balanced I forget that I'm hood.
Laugh at myself how grown I've become.
Thankful for her hospitality because I know where she from.
We cut from a cloth that doesn't exist anymore.
Blessings from God keep us both on the board.
What I see and she saw it's a beautiful thing.
Out my pocket surprise her a gold diamond ring.

YOU ARE

So cool so fly so nice of you to see.
Live life in gods' eyes explore some possibilities.
At the same time respect a true friendship bond.
Without raising alarms, enjoy each other lucky charm.
Communicate well with a high scale indigo.
Learned to let things go and show the world how I flow.
When im in flight above clouds, it's a different type of height.
My site follows bright lights that shine on nights.
Something happened to me got me feeling groovy.
As if im starring in a movie, called she's the one for me.
The natural occurrence is keeping tone and language
balanced.
Never hungry for that love affectionate, warm sandwich.
So well prepared , still aware of the contents.
Here you go take a sip of something sweet healthy and honest.
Not an afraid to make a promise for the love of god any.
I always return to the point from which they send me

www.ingramcontent.com/pod-product-compliance
Lightning Source LLC
Chambersburg PA
CBHW071652040426
42452CB00009B/1839